TAKE M

MAKE IT (12)
BREAK

TAKE MY HEART AND

MAKE IT BREAK

The Pursuit and Rescue

of a Man Running from God

STEVE SHANKS

TATE PUBLISHING
AND ENTERPRISES, LLC

Make it Break
Copyright © 2011 by Steve Shanks. All rights reserved.

No part of this publication may be reproduced, stored in a retrieval system or transmitted in any way by any means, electronic, mechanical, photocopy, recording or otherwise without the prior permission of the author except as provided by USA copyright law.

Scriptures taken from the *Holy Bible, New International Version*®, niv®. Copyright © 1973, 1978, 1984 by Biblica, Inc.™ Used by permission of Zondervan. All rights reserved worldwide. www.zondervan.com

The opinions expressed by the author are not necessarily those of Tate Publishing, LLC.

Published by Tate Publishing & Enterprises, LLC
127 E. Trade Center Terrace | Mustang, Oklahoma 73064 USA
1.888.361.9473 | www.tatepublishing.com

Tate Publishing is committed to excellence in the publishing industry. The company reflects the philosophy established by the founders, based on Psalm 68:11,
"The Lord gave the word and great was the company of those who published it."

Book design copyright © 2011 by Tate Publishing, LLC. All rights reserved.
Cover design by Blake Brasor
Interior design by Chelsea Womble

Published in the United States of America

ISBN: 978-1-61346-748-0
1. Biography & Autobiography / Religious
2. Biography & Autobiography / Personal Memoirs
11.11.02

I would like to dedicate this book to Michelle, Adam, Nolan, and Cara. Thank you for your unconditional love, forgiveness, patience, and trust.

TABLE OF
CONTENTS

PREFACE

But Jonah ran away from the Lord and headed
for Tarshish.

Jonah 1:3 (NIV)

This is a story about an ordinary man who rejected
God and wanted to live his own way. God let him go
on his own prideful path, then pursued him and eventually broke him in a very public way. The man didn't
deserve mercy, but that is what he received. The man
didn't deserve any love and grace, but that is all he has
experienced since he started to believe.

THE END OF
ONE LIFE

At 5:15 A.M. on Wednesday, May 17, 2006, I got out of bed in Clive, Iowa, and quietly went downstairs to get the paper. My wife Michelle got out of her side of the bed and followed me without saying a word. We hadn't talked or slept at all through the night. I felt her presence behind me as I walked toward the kitchen with the *Des Moines Register* newspaper in my hands. I went to the front of the sports page and saw the article about me. I did not want to read the article. I handed the paper to Michelle for her to read.

After a few minutes of forehead rubbing at the kitchen counter I said, "How bad is it...scale of one to ten?"

Michelle was sitting in a chair in the living room under a light.

After a horribly long pause, she replied quietly, "Ten."

I put my head down into my cold, sweaty, and trembling hands. My life, as I knew it, was over. I was a successful teacher, coach, and school administrator. I was almost to the end of a rewarding first year in my dream job as the athletic director of the prestigious Dowling Catholic High School in West Des Moines, Iowa. But now, I was on the sports page because of something that had nothing to do with sports.

Later that day, my story was the top story on the ten o'clock news. News anchors on two of the three central Iowa television stations were starting their broadcasts with my shocking story. By Saturday, three painful days later, my resignation was on the front page, top fold right. I felt like I was being gutted and hung on a hook. Now, my twenty-two-year career in education was gone because of a self-centered, atheistic mind-set, an "errant" e-mail, and one anvil of a news article.

Not that I didn't have it coming.

FOUNDATIONS

I grew up as the fifth of five boys in the Robert and Mary Shanks family. My dad was a hog buyer for Hormel and my mom stayed home and took care of the family. We moved from time to time because dad would get transferred. I was born in Spencer, Iowa, and grew up in Fort Dodge, Iowa.

Mom grew up in Windom, Minnesota. The Bunkers were staunch Catholics and had a very big family. My dad was an only child and grew up in central Missouri. The Shankses originally were herdsman that came out of Scotland. Granddad Shanks landed in Missouri and managed several black angus herds while raising my dad. In the summer of 1949, Bob Shanks of Missouri and Mary Bunkers of Minnesota met at Yellowstone Park, Wyoming. They were part of the summer work crew that the park had hired.

They fell in love, married, and raised five boys. Dad converted to Catholicism and we were all raised in the Catholic faith. I was educated in Fort Dodge's St. Edmond Catholic school system. I was a typical teen in terms of my religion. I prayed once in a while but didn't have a close relationship with God despite being in a school system based on religion.

Religion and spirituality were never really personalized for me until I was around twelve years old. My brother Dave, who is ten years older than me, grew up at the end of the hippy and Vietnam War era. He got into drugs and was leading a life spiraling downward when he became a believer in God and was "born again." He came home to Fort Dodge after being saved and he scared the heck out of me. His religious fervor repelled me from spirituality.

A few years later, our high school basketball team made it to the state tournament at Vets Auditorium in Des Moines. We were all incredibly excited as we got off the bus and headed in to play our first round opponent. As the team was walking up the steps to the front doors of the big auditorium, in the cold of early March, I saw my born-again brother Dave with his long hair, beard, and an armful of "New Life

Center" newspapers. I was an immature teenager and I was totally embarrassed by how my brother looked and by how he was acting. I turned the other way so that he wouldn't see me and walked into the building, completely ignoring my own brother. I didn't want my peers to know that the "Jesus freak" at the doorway was my own flesh and blood! I was seeing how God was affecting my brother and I was filtering that information through my immature eyes and the final image was very negative. The foundation of my belief that God was for weird or weak people was being formed. It's that foundation of belief, along with my self-centered nature, that would lead me, one day, into my own downward spiral.

A LUKEWARM CHRISTIAN BECOMES A CATHOLIC SCHOOL ADMINISTRATOR

After high school, I went to Iowa State University in Ames and pursued a career in teaching and coaching. I met my future wife, Michelle, during my last year at the university. We connected as we were both singing to Bruce Springsteen's song "Pink Cadillac" on top of chairs at the Hayloft Lounge in Fort Dodge, Iowa. We've been together ever since.

My first teaching job was in northwest Iowa in the farming community of Correctionville and Cushing, Iowa, and the Eastwood Community School District. Michelle and I got married in 1988 and started to raise a family while I coached four sports and she worked as a medical assistant in a doctor's office in Sioux City.

Adam was born in 1990. We moved to Moville, Iowa, soon after Adam's birth. Moville is a very nice small town fifteen miles east of Sioux City. We wanted to live there because we liked the small-town lifestyle, and the distance made for a shorter commute for Michelle. Nolan was born in 1993 and Cara rounded out the lineup in 1995. After I got a job teaching in Sioux City, Michelle and I both commuted to work while our kids stayed in Moville, fifteen miles away, either at the Woodbury Central elementary school or at the babysitter. Life was pretty good. I had success as a high school baseball coach and was moving up the ladder in the Sioux City Community School District. I was anxious to keep moving. I worked toward a degree in school administration and dreamed of being a big-school athletic director. I eventually became an assistant principal at Sioux City East while still coaching baseball.

After two years as a big-school administrator, the secondary principal's position opened at a small Catholic high school in LeMars, Iowa. LeMars is a very nice town of about 10,000 people and is known as the home of Blue Bunny Ice Cream. Gehlen Catholic needed a principal. I was interested in getting our kids into a Catholic school system like Michelle and I had experienced, so I applied. Gehlen was looking for someone with a strong track record who would be willing to make a long-term commitment to the school. I had what they wanted and I got the job. Our family moved twenty-five miles north and our three kids enrolled in their first Catholic school. We felt like we were moving to a big city because LeMars had fast food restaurants and a movie theater! I also felt that this move was our last move and that we would retire in LeMars.

When I took this position, I tried to commit myself to deepening my Catholic faith. My spiritual life had been a rollercoaster that had even delved into non-belief. I had often thought, during my college years, that God didn't exist because the planet earth just happened to be the right distance from the sun to sustain life and that we were all just a part of evolution. Because of my experiences with my born-again brother, I felt that God was for weak people who couldn't handle life and had to "give all their worries to the 'Lord.'" I remember being in a bar with friends arguing about the existence of God. My buddies were very surprised that the son of Mary Shanks and a graduate of St. Edmond High School believed that God was a fictional crutch for weak people.

But now, it was time to be a leader in a Catholic school. I had to get serious about my faith. I felt I could do it because I had grown up in a Catholic school system, and I was able to thrive there without making a serious commitment to God. *If I just try*, I thought, *I could really be a strong leader in this religion-based school system.* Therefore, I looked at my religion as part of my job description. Getting connected to God became an item on my to-do lists. Not exactly the way to go about it, but that's where I was as a lukewarm, and frequently doubting Christian.

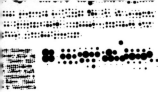

A VOICE IN THE AISLE

I have summoned you by name; you are mine.
Isaiah 43:1

Next to Gehlen Catholic School is St. Joseph's Church. St. Joe's is a beautiful and very old church. During my first two years as principal, I would sneak over to the church a couple of times a month during the school day to pray, meditate, and get away from the busyness of the school. The job of school administrator can be very challenging. Private-school administrators have an extra challenge in respects to parents having to pay tuition. It's an incredible challenge balancing a fair salary for the teachers with affordable tuition for the students. I often felt connected to God during those times of challenge at Gehlen.

My prayer life, though still weak, improved. I truly believed in the goodness of our little school.

I wanted to see enrollment rise and I believed that the best way to increase enrollment was to provide a strong Christian and academic atmosphere for young people. The school's image, which had taken a hit before I arrived, began to improve, and with the help of a lot of people, things began to fall in place.

Also, something incredible happened to me at St. Joe's on a Sunday in October 2004. I had just received communion from our parish priest and was turning the corner on my walk back to my pew when I heard someone literally call my name, "Steve." It sounded as if it came from inside my head. I stopped in my tracks for a quick moment and I looked hard left and right. I didn't recognize anyone. If someone had called my name, wouldn't they be looking at me waiting for me to look and give a smile back at them? No one was looking at me from either side.

It was a deep male voice and it was as clear as day. *It had to be someone who knew me in those first couple of rows*, I thought to myself as I found my pew and kneeled back down. From my knees, I looked back to the corner where I had heard someone call my name.

I thought, *Could that have been God?* I put my face into my hands and shook my head. *Was I just literally "called by name" like it's written about in the Bible and sung in church hymns?* I wondered feverishly. I didn't tell Michelle or anyone else. I was hoping that God really did connect with me. At the same time, I was scared to death about the commitment that would be asked of me if He had indeed made an appearance at St. Joe's on my behalf that Sunday morning. I wasn't ready for that. I wasn't ready to make a life changing commitment.

I also knew that what had happened was not part of my imagination. I hadn't had a "feeling" or "a sense" that it had happened; it really happened. But, when it comes to opportunities in my life, I haven't always been wise with my decisions. Instead of embracing what had happened and sharing it with my family and colleagues, I ran away from what had happened. I ran away because I knew that a full commitment to Christ would change everything about the life that I was enjoying, and it would radically change the way that people looked at me.

A CHANGE IN THE WIND

Our little family was in LeMars for three years when, in the spring of 2005, I got a call from the head baseball coach at Dowling Catholic High School in West Des Moines, Iowa. Dowling is the largest Catholic school in the state of Iowa. For Catholics interested in Catholic schools, Dowling is seen as prestigious; a place with a history of athletic success. I looked at Dowling as the "mansion on the hill" and had, for years, told my brother and a few close friends that I would love to be the athletic director at Dowling. I knew that I would apply when their long-time A.D. retired.

I had coached baseball against Tim, the head varsity coach at Dowling, when he was coaching at Heelan Catholic in Sioux City. He told me that the athletic director job at Dowling was coming open and he thought I should apply. I was ecstatic. I felt like I had a shot at the position because of my administrative experience, coaching background, and my affiliation with Catholic schools.

Not only that, but the president of Dowling just happened to be an alumnus of Gehlen Catholic High School in LeMars. I met him at Gehlen's 50th anniversary ball about a month before I knew that the A.D. position at Dowling would be open.

I was extremely nervous coming into this all-school reunion event because I had to give a state- of- the-union type speech about Gehlen and talk about the benefits of Catholic education. The speech went well. I walked over to Dowling's president after the dinner was over. I wanted to say to him, "Hey, if you're athletic director job ever comes open, I'd be interested." I didn't have the courage to make that statement, but I was intrigued that this connection between Gehlen and Dowling existed.

Our three kids had, of course, been growing up in small town northwest Iowa, riding bikes to their friend's houses and to the pool. Michelle loved her job even though it meant a daily commute to Sioux

City. We had a nice house and we were very happy. But "Hey," I said to myself, "this is Dowling. I have to at least give it a shot."

Michelle knew how badly I wanted to be the athletic director at Dowling, but she didn't say very much when I officially applied. After I got the call to go to West Des Moines for the interview, she did say, "We are happy here. I love my job and the kids are happy." I could rationalize that away and did so rather quickly. "We'll be happier in a larger city, honey," I replied and added, "Our family is in central Iowa (that will hit its target). There are a lot more things to do and our kids will love it." And then, I threw in the big ammo that contained a little fate and divine purpose, "Michelle, the president of Dowling was at the Ball! He went to Gehlen Catholic High School. If that's not a sign then I don't know what is."

I was using God to my self-centered advantage. Maybe He was letting me be me in order to push that first domino down. I told Michelle that this was our destiny. I wanted to feel guilt-free about this opportunity. I went to St. Joe's one Saturday morning, after taking our dog for a run, to pray, meditate, and ask God for direction. I wanted His approval but I only stayed for a minute or two and then I left. I wasn't feeling it spiritually. When I started to pray (because that's what I was supposed to do), the feelings that I would start to get didn't jive with the direction I knew I wanted to take. I don't think I liked the answers that were about to come from a conversation with God. The answers that *were* coming out of my own inner reflection *were* real.

I knew that Gehlen would offer my kids more opportunities in sports and fine arts than Dowling could offer. There would be a ton of academic and extracurricular competition there. I wanted my kids to play all the sports. Would they be talented enough to play for one of the best high school athletic programs in the state? Somehow, I worked around that equation and buried reality. My train of thought was this: *If they worked really hard, they should be able to make any team. And if they didn't work hard, then they wouldn't make the team and that's okay; maybe they shouldn't be playing that particular sport anyway.* That, to me, is one of the saddest things about my state of mind at that time. I pushed aside what was best for my own children in pursuit of my career.

I also knew Gehlen needed me more than Dowling did. Dowling could find many good people to take that A.D. job. The president of Gehlen Catholic, who is a Catholic priest, wanted Dowling to hire someone besides me. When I told him what was happening, he called me (now, he laughed *a little* when he said this) a "shithead." I was taken aback. A priest just called me a "shithead!" *He was right!* We, at Gehlen, had just hired a great development director and the three of us were poised to do some good things together. Father was angry at me. I brushed his feelings aside because they were standing in the way of the Dowling job.

Instead of connecting with God, my boss, my spouse, or my kids in making this huge decision, I consulted my friends. They, like me, knew that this kind of opportunity might be once in a lifetime. Looking back, I only sought the advice of those who I knew would agree with me.

After my interview in West Des Moines, I got the offer from Dowling's president and I asked for a few days to think about it. I couldn't believe this was happening. I took our big yellow dog to the school's practice track and football field to jog, walk, and think about the job offer, and what we had personally and professionally in LeMars. After a few laps, I stopped and put both hands on my knees and began to sob, my shoulders shaking. I had never cried so hard before. The school that I was working at was a nice little Catholic school with great people. They had put their trust in me, paying me more than any principal before in order to draw me out of a big public high school in Sioux City. I had just completed three successful years. It was a hard job at Gehlen, but it had many rewards involving things that really mattered.

My emotions flooded out on that practice field. I fell to one knee and looked through my soaked eyes to see if anyone was watching.

It's taken me awhile to fully understand why I was crying so hard. At the time, I wasn't sure what was going on. I know now, however, that I was running from what I knew in my heart was right. I was running from the spiritual opportunity that Gehlen and St. Joseph's Church offered me. I was turning my back on what was right for my family. I was running from God.

Just like Jonah ran from God before being swallowed up by a whale, I was running from everything spiritual in order to be the A.D. at Dowling. I hadn't told them "yes" yet, but I knew what my answer was going to be. I wept because I knew that I was betraying my family, my school, and everything spiritual. On paper, the obvious decision was to not take this gig in West Des Moines. If I made one of those lists that experts say you should do when you have to make a big decision (the two column chart with the pros and cons), my chart would have had everything right and true on one side, and "Dream Job" and "Prestige" on the other. In my mind, the one truth outweighed all the others. I called Dowling's president and accepted the offer.

Within a few hours, I was strategizing how to tell the kids about our impending move to the big city. It had just been three years since we ripped them out of Moville to come up to a bigger small town. And now, they were very happy. I decided to divide and conquer. I didn't want to have a family meeting like the one we had in Moville three years earlier where Adam teetered into the cushions of the couch and cried (which made the little ones cry even though they didn't fully understand).

Instead, I shot hoops with Adam, a sophomore to be, in the school gym and sat him down to talk about my great opportunity. I told him how Gehlen may have to go to one K-12 administrator instead of two (which was true based on that always-tight budget, but I was pushing it a little). I took Nolan, twelve years old at the time, out for a walk along a creek on the west edge of town with Benny our dog. I told him about all the great things to do in central Iowa. Nine-year-old Cara, my baby girl, liked to go down to the school and rollerblade around the parking lot while I worked out in Gehlen's tiny weight room. After a quick workout, I sat her on the tailgate of my pickup truck and told her that we would still be able to come back and see her friends. Cara cried pretty hard. We got back into the truck and drove back home.

In the end, I was proud of myself for how well the news was absorbed. I avoided the mass wailing that would have happened in a big family meeting. Rationalization had taken over any slivers of conscience that I had left. A conversation with God was now the last thing on my mind. Nothing was going to interfere with me becoming the A.D. at Dowling. I made sure of that.

So, after fourteen years as a middle school social studies teacher, two years as an assistant principal at Sioux City East High School, three years as the secondary principal at LeMars Gehlen Catholic High School in LeMars, Iowa, and twenty summers as a high school baseball coach, I became the athletic director at Iowa's most high-profile Catholic high school in West Des Moines, Iowa.

And my wife and three kids were coming along for the ride.

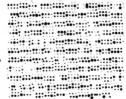

HEADING TOWARD THE CLIFF

Despite leaving a lot of great things in northwest Iowa, life in the big city was good. The school's baseball team moved us into our new house on Clark Street in Clive and the kids got off to a good start in school. The job at Dowling was very challenging and immediately rewarding.

Leading Dowling Catholic High School Athletics was, to me, the ultimate job for a Catholic kid who loved high school athletics. Being the Dowling A.D. meant that I had a chance to lead a big-time high school program that had won, at that time, twenty-eight state championships in various sports. As I took the job, one of my old high school friends weighed in. He said, "The Dowling A.D. job is the toughest job in the state of Iowa." I thought he was blowing smoke. I did know, however, that I was entering a sports program with nineteen sports, seventeen of them with their own independent booster club. It was a school with high tuition and high expectations for success. When parents pay big money for tuition, many times, they want a return for their investment—which means, of course, playing time.

Despite both the real and perceived pressure of the job, I felt at home; like being an athletic director in a big school like Dowling was my calling. My plan was to reinvent our booster club structure and improve the quality of our coaching and athletic facilities. I enjoyed my status in the big market. I was on TV once in awhile and people were taking me out for lunch! On the same day that I started my new job, I threw out the first pitch at a Dowling baseball game being played at Principal Park, home of the Triple-A Iowa Cubs. My kids were proud of their dad, and I was proud of myself.

During my first month or so at Dowling, I would start the day by trying to be one of the first people in the school building and going into the school chapel. I'd say a prayer or two to help me get a good start to the day. Part of me wanted to do the right thing and make sure that the athletic department was visibly Christ-centered (a phrase that is in the school's mission statement) in an obvious way. I was trying to follow the mission of the school. But it didn't take long for the demands of the job and my own spiritual doubts to end that morning ritual.

Going to church also became more and more of a struggle as the winter sports seasons started. My doubts of the existence of God became more and more pervasive. Ironically, it was during mass that I questioned God the most. I complained internally about various parts of the Catholic mass. I questioned the Bible, especially the story of Jesus's birth and resurrection. Once again, rationalization became my theme. I would explain away Jesus's miracles as embellished stories. I became convinced that Jesus was just a man, and the resurrection was a fabrication. I squirmed when it was time for the second reading in the Catholic mass—a scripture reading from the letters of St. Paul. I hated that second reading. To me, Paul's writings were gibberish, and I tuned that part of the mass completely out.

Also, the songs at church went on too long for my liking. I was becoming more and more bitter toward my religion. These negative feelings coincided with the increasing stress, time, and effort that it was taking to run a large and deeply political high school athletic department.

Although things were going well professionally, the job that I had was consuming me. The mission of the school didn't jive with the politics. The realities of the A.D. position were frustrating me, and asking God for help wasn't a consideration. I was doing everything by myself. At home at night, when there wasn't a game to be at, I started reading internet articles about how God was becoming less popular in the age of technology. I started to consciously search the internet for evidence that God didn't exist. I started to bury whatever religion I had in my life with a big metal shovel.

So there I was, a Catholic school athletic director during the day; wearing my tie, working next to the crucifix on the wall, participating in group prayers before meetings, going to mass in the Dowling gym, and then going home to feed myself information that fought against the very existence of God. In January and February of 2006, I became a hardened atheist who couldn't wait to read the next magazine article written by some intellectual convinced that religion and God were inventions of weak and stupid men. There was a force driving me in this direction. It was like having a food craving; I couldn't help myself to enough written material about atheism in order to justify the way I was feeling.

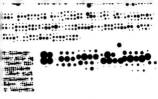

SEALING THE DEAL
WITH A SONG

In February 2006, I became emotionally attached to a Sheryl Crow song called "Letter to God." It's on her *Wildflower* CD. I have always loved her music because of her intense lyrics about love, but this song came at me with a different slant. The song is critical of organized religion and expresses hope as well as some doubts about the existence of God. It was right in my psychological wheelhouse because of what I perceived as ambiguity. The lyrics were like rocket fuel to my fire of spiritual doubt.

I played this song over and over everywhere I went in our 1998 Toyota Sienna minivan for weeks. *For weeks!* To work and back, to pick up a pizza for dinner, on the way to a game. Not if the kids were in the car because they would ask questions. I was using

41

this song as my own personal referendum for God's existence. Just as I rationalized my way to the big city, I was rationalizing God out of my life. My brain was working the equation toward total disbelief in God. A whole life surrounded by the Catholic religion was being deleted from my belief system. I look back now and think about how I was so hooked into that song. It's an intense song and it was thumping me like a hammer in the middle of my forehead. Now, five-years later, I am convinced that it was God moving my heart toward the precipice. "Letter to God" sealed the deal for me. I was done with religion. That song was literally the only song on my playlist as the winter sports season was nearing its conclusion.

It may not be what Ms. Crow meant to deliver when she wrote the lyrics, but, for me, her song was like a brick on the accelerator as I was driving my life's bus toward a cliff.

THE E-MAIL

February 2006 was ugly for me. My hours at basketball, wrestling and swimming events were increasing. There was pressure to not renew the contracts of the head wrestling coach and head boys basketball coach. The plan for a new booster club structure was taking shape, and it was going to really shake things up with parents and benefactors. I was drinking more alcohol at night and brushing up on the latest magazine articles on intellectualism and atheism. I somehow was convincing myself that I could be an administrator at a private school based on faith in God and not believe in God. My attitude toward my job was hardening (probably in preparation for some big decisions that had to be made). My heart was hardening. My life was hardening.

Pastor Alistair Begg of Parkside Church in Cleveland, Ohio says, "The course of disobedience is always down until the Lord intervenes."[1] The course I was on was definitely down. Another typical behavior when a person runs from God is the total reliance on self. I started to insulate myself from my family and my co-workers. As athletic director, I was doing too much on my own without consulting anyone else in school administration. Big decisions were on their way, and instead of trying to build any consensus, I was acting more like a lone wolf.

We hosted the Class 4A District Wrestling meet on a Saturday in February. It was the first time Dowling had hosted a district meet in several years and I really wanted to put on a great event. That evening, my fourth grade daughter Cara was looking forward to the Holy Trinity (the K-8th grade school Nolan and Cara attended) Father-Daughter Dance in downtown Des Moines. I knew the wrestling meet would last all day, but I promised Cara that it wouldn't interfere with the start of the dance.

It did.

I was late getting home. Cara, dressed like a little princess, was waiting semi-patiently. Michelle wasn't so patient. The look she gave me when I came through the door said everything. I changed quickly and off Cara and I went. We got to the dance late, but Cara was still pumped. I, however, had a problem. As host of the wrestling meet, we had to report the results to the state's athletic association. Our faxes from the wrestling coaches weren't going through and an official from the athletic association was calling me on my cell phone. I had to leave the dance and my daughter four separate times during the dance in order to find a quiet spot while I called the coach and tried to reassure the official. Cara kept asking, "Daddy, where do you keep going?" I was exhausted and feeling pressure from all angles.

If my priorities were right I would have been the father that I needed to be that night. Instead, I was worried more about my image as the athletic director. Being perceived as disorganized because we weren't getting the wrestling results to the association on time was burning me up. My attitude toward the Father-Daughter dance wasn't good.

I was also exhausted because the winter sports season was taking its toll. I had spent around seventy hours the previous week at school or at athletic events. Although the sports teams were mostly successful, there was always parental pressure based on playing time or coaching strategy. Sunday's worship service only added more weight onto the gas pedal. I went to work extra early Monday morning, walked past the chapel, and opened up my office to clear the mess left from the crazy week before.

I started the day by looking at several e-mails. First, I responded to an e-mail from my brother Joe. Joe was, and still is, a Catholic school athletic director. We are close and frequently give each other grief as well as vent the frustrations of our jobs.

I wrote a reply to him that led off with "I'm done with religion" and how much I hated my parish's "long-ass" homilies. Talking religion wasn't a normal topic of conversation for my brother and I but that's what was on my mind. I complained of the "long-ass" singing and made fun of how our pastor looked, writing that he reminded me of a member of the mafia. I went on to complain to my brother that the parent booster club for girls basketball were "idiots" since they had "f***ed up" (exact letters and asterisks used in the e-mail) their state tourney t-shirts because the shirts weren't in school colors.

Now *by itself*, the e-mail was an insulting, disrespectful, and unprofessional communication on any computer, let alone a school computer. But this *wasn't by itself*. God was arranging a pretty perfect storm. I pushed the send button and glanced at the address box at the same time. The e-mail, which I thought was a simple reply to my brother, somehow had the e-mail address of the wife of Dowling's head boy's basketball coach on it. I had been flipping back and forth between e-mails. I don't know how the address of a reply e-mail to my brother had changed but it had. A few hours after I had pushed send, I received a reply from her which read, "Are you sure you meant this for me?" I felt a little embarrassed and reviewed what I had written in the e-mail. "Not that big of a deal. Don't worry about it," was my conclusion. I didn't know it yet but my fate as the A.D. at Dowling was pretty much sealed that morning with that "errant e-mail" (as the newspaper would later describe it).

A few weeks after the e-mail was sent and forgotten about (at least by me), I told our head varsity basketball coach that his contract would not be renewed. The coach that was let go also had possession of my inappropriate e-mail. He was from, and lived in Des Moines's south side, a section of the city that is proud of its Italian heritage. Many "Southsiders" were already upset with Dowling for personnel moves in prior years that they felt excluded people who were their neighbors and who they respected.

The way I handled his non-renewal was strange and wrong. At that point in my professional life, I had dealt with at least five non-renewals or firings. I know enough about human nature and respecting others that I had always let employees go in a face-to-face meeting. There is no other way to let someone go. Not by letter, e-mail, or phone call. Not by a proxy or underling. I have never even considered firing someone over the phone because it is unprofessional; except this time with this coach. I had met with him on two occasions, post-season, prior to letting him go. We talked about the program and the negative things that were happening. He probably knew where I was going and I hoped that he would resign to "spend more time with his family." When the decision to let him go was solid in my brain and in my heart, I decided to tell him. But I had an overwhelming urge to tell him over the phone. Part of me couldn't believe that I was thinking this way, but a bigger part of me said that I *had to* handle this thing over the phone. It was the wrong thing to do. I'm sure the coach and his friends used the phone call firing to their advantage and well, they should have. It's something that I had never done before and wouldn't consider doing again. But in the spring of 2006, it was a part of the perfect storm. I don't doubt that God planted that urge to make a phone call because a meeting might have had a different result than the phone call did.

The e-mail was sent as the school was preparing to start a big capital campaign to raise millions of dollars for structural renovations. The development director was making preparations to visit with the big donors, millionaires who are sensitive to the image of the school and who would hold the key to any fundraising effort. The e-mail was sent as we were pushing for big changes in the booster club apparatus. We were moving from seventeen separate sport booster clubs to one. Toes were being stepped on. Parents involved in the high profile sports were going to have to share resources with the lower profile sports that didn't have a strong booster club. And the south side of Des Moines just needed a spark in order to create a fire at the school.

Another part of the landscape was The *Des Moines Register*, Iowa's biggest newspaper. Its sports section is known for having a very aggressive investigative reporter who digs into public or private official's missteps like a dog down a gopher hole. He has a powerful writing style and he has a knack for putting facts into their worst possible light. If he was writing a story about you, you might as well clean off your desk and leave your keys.

Throw red meat to any of these groups individually and you have a problem. Give them all something to chew on at the same time and you have the potential for a massacre. I believe that God had all the pieces in place for me to drop into an abyss. I ran from Him and He chased me and created a perfect storm of circumstances that would lead to my fall. Alistair Begg says that, "The devil will always have a conveyance waiting for you when you're determined to run away from the presence of the Lord," and that "He (the devil) may provide the ride but you will pay the fare."[2]

I was about to pay the fare. All I had to do was to press "Send."

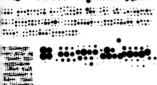

PAYING THE FARE

From inside the fish, Jonah prayed…You hurled me into the deep, into the very heart of the seas, and the currents swirled about me.

Jonah 2:1, 3

About a week after the news broke about the basketball coach (this was six weeks after I had hit the button to send the e-mail) I got a call on my cell phone from a radio personality who broadcasted Dowling games and coached in the basketball program at Dowling.

He asked me if I remembered sending an e-mail to the wife of the coach. "No," I replied as I tried to remember.

"You said some things about a parish priest that really has some people upset," he said.

A lump landed in my throat even before I fully remembered what he was referring to. Having people upset at me for any reason has always hit me hard. I was immediately scared. I walked back to my office and went through my old e-mails. It all came back. I asked myself, "Could this be that big of a deal?" It was.

My boss, the Gehlen alum, brought me in the next day. He had a copy of the e-mail. The basketball coach and his wife had met with him a day or two earlier. They asked him how Dowling could employ a man like me.

I told the president that it was mostly a joke with my brother, but that I had meant a few of the things I wrote. It was shaded truth. He was supportive, but I knew he was not happy.

Wheels started to turn. The supporters of the basketball coach and others upset by the content of the e-mail were sending it around town and feeding it to the newspaper. I kept things to myself and didn't tell Michelle for a week or two. After having more and more tense conversations with the president of Dowling and his crisis management specialist, I became more and more anxious. I told Michelle about the e-mail, framing it so that it came out as positive as possible, and she reassured me that it would be okay. One Dowling supporter wrote a letter to the president saying that I should have to go to sensitivity training. That didn't sound so bad. I didn't believe for a second that my job was in jeopardy...yet. I was just hoping that it wouldn't land in the state's largest newspaper.

A couple of days later, I was in a meeting with the high school principal when the president of the school called me out to the hallway and told me that "the" reporter from the Des Moines Register wanted to talk to him about the e-mail. He showed me a note given to him by his secretary with the reporter's last name on it. That was it. My heart, lungs, and liver sank to the carpet of the Dowling administrative offices.

I told Michelle about the Register reporter and waited for the paper to contact me. The president and the reporter met and had a short conversation. Television reporters started to hover around the school. No one from the Register talked to me but the Register ran the story anyway on Wednesday, May 17, on the front page of the sports section the next morning. Like Michelle said, the article was a "ten" in terms of its power. Although the article had some factual errors concerning what I had written in the e-mail, it didn't matter. It wouldn't have mattered if the article was factually correct or not. Either way, I was cooked because of what I wrote about our parish priest and my phrase, "I'm done with religion."

The article contained quotes from the brother of the priest that I had chastised. The brother said that he wouldn't want his grandchildren to go to Dowling if people like me were employed there.

E-mails came in to my office in support of me including a nice call from Iowa State University's football coach who had been the subject of a tough article in the same paper years earlier. He offered support and shared his feelings about the same news reporter who wrote that article. I felt buoyed by the support I was getting, but there was no way of changing the path of the storm. A special school board meeting to discuss the situation was scheduled for Thursday night. Dowling's president called me before the board meeting and asked me to be in his office at 9:30 A.M. Friday morning. He also indicated that I didn't have to come to the board meeting. I've always been a bit naïve and trusting (qualities I got from my mom) so I didn't get the meaning of the Friday morning meeting. I actually had hope that I was going to be suspended for awhile but nothing more. In reality, my fate was probably sealed before the Dowling school board even discussed the issue that night.

Trying to keep things under control, I took the kids to school Friday morning, stopping at a convenience store to get them a donut for the trip to Holy Trinity. My best friend from Fort Dodge, now a lawyer in Phoenix, called me on my cell phone while I was in line to ask how things were going. I told him about the school board meeting the night before where several people spoke on my behalf. I was upbeat until I told him that I had a meeting with the school president set for 9:30 A.M. that morning.

"Oh," he replied. Silence followed. His tone was dark and had obvious meaning. Being a lawyer, he knew the purpose of such meetings and had seen them go down many times before. I now realized the worst may be about to happen. My friend's reaction put a lump in my throat the size of a softball. I put my donut-free hand on my forehead and thought, *"Man, I've been in education for twenty years. I've always been praised and I've been successful as a teacher, coach and administrator…"* Despite that, and because of my own actions, the ax was about to drop.

My kids were talking to me on the way from the convenience store to the school, but I was falling into a state of shock. Couldn't the school say, "Steve's a good man; He made a mistake but we're going to work through this." *Suspend me*, I thought. "Send me to sensitivity training," I said to myself.

After dropping the kids off at Holy Trinity, I went to an empty ballpark parking lot in Urbandale, Iowa, and parked the minivan. It was about an hour before my meeting. Becoming totally numb, I played a song from a Bob Schneider live recording titled "F*** 'em" about how when things go bad, well…you know. I played it over and over, from the parking lot where I stewed until 9:10 A.M. to my parking spot at the school. It was my last prideful stand against the tsunami rushing towards me.

I wasn't going to get it. Although I had apologized personally twice to my parish priest who I chastised in the e-mail and to the president of the girls basketball booster club a week earlier, I hadn't tried to connect with God to ask for forgiveness and guidance. He wasn't on my radar. I was still trying to handle this debacle on my own.

God knew what it would take to get my attention though. All of the thunder clouds were gathering in the office of the school's president. I entered his office at exactly 9:30 A.M. Dowling's school board president and the school's crisis lawyer were in the room as well. As I remember, everyone was dressed in mostly black…including me.

"Steve, the feedback in this deal has just been too much," Dowling's president said.

What an incredible experience to feel the trap door being released from under you and the rope snapping your neck.

I didn't say a whole lot. I was numb. It was suggested that I step down at the end of the school day in front of staff in the school's library or auditorium. I didn't want to have any part of that. This wasn't happening. It had to be a bad dream. It was so public and so embarrassing.

Between the much needed donors for the capital campaign, offended booster club members, the brother of the priest who was quoted in the paper saying he couldn't send his grandchildren to Dowling if I was there, and backers of the former basketball coach, I was forced to resign. There was no forgiveness for the crude and errant e-mail out of the Catholic school or our parish (which I would have welcomed then but am grateful for now). It was Friday, May 19, 2006, and I was done. It was a major news story in the state, and a husband-and-father-administered punch in the gut to my wife and kids.

I went from being a prominent administrator at two high schools based on the Catholic religion to a total nonbeliever. And as I ran away from God, He chased me. After watching all my silliness, it was as if God had had enough and said "*Take his heart and make it break* so he can become useful again."

Jonah of the Bible had to pay a fare to get on that boat as he ran from God's will. Now, I had to pay a fare. The "Fare," to me, was the public embarrassment. It was the loss of employment and the decimation of my reputation that the e-mail had caused—something that I wouldn't wish on anyone. It was also a betrayal to Michelle and the kids, who supported me in this adventure even though their hearts were still in LeMars, Iowa. The "Fare" was also complete brokenness—something, however painful, that I needed in a big way.

AFTERSHOCK

There is no one so great or mighty that he can avoid the misery that will rise up against him when he resists and strives against God.

—John Calvin

After the 9:30 A.M. hanging in the president's office, I went home to Michelle. I met her at the bottom of the stairs where she had come down from her home office and said, "They let me go." She grabbed my head from the second step where she stood and brought me into her chest. Her support was unreal. I walked around in a daze trying to speak. She called Dowling and had the dean of students get my freshman son out of class. Adam then picked up our other two kids who were told that their brother was on his way to pick them up at Holy Trinity School. They didn't deserve to have that twenty-minute car ride from Holy

Trinity to Clark Street on their own, knowing something big and bad was happening. The kids arrived at home about 10:30 A.M. and walked into the kitchen wide-eyed.

Telling your kids that you messed up so bad that you lost your job is not an easy thing to do. I was so embarrassed personally, and sad for them because I knew what they would face at school until the end of the year. I had ripped them out of Mayberry. I had knowingly put them in a school situation where they wouldn't have that small school ability to participate in everything. This move had completely changed Michelle's direction professionally; all for me and this dream job to be at the biggest Catholic high school in the state. And now this was happening.

I didn't have a lawyer or a public relations person. I called my brother Joe and he said that he was on his way to our house. I called my lawyer friend from Phoenix, the best man in our wedding and he gave me good advice on how to handle my letter of resignation. Dowling asked me to come back to school at three thirty and read my letter of resignation to the faculty and probably news reporters. I declined again. Making a public apology may have been a good thing to do. It may have helped my recovery. Or it may have been a fiasco. All I know is that I couldn't bring myself to go back to the school.

My brother Joe and I got in the car to go get some food. His car's radio was tuned to the local sports talk radio station. Some caller was disparaging me and my e-mail embolism. We listened to his entire rant. Neither of us said much and I turned the channel.

I picked up the paper at my doorstep Saturday morning and saw my name and picture at the top of the front page. I didn't read the article. I threw the newspaper into the coat closet. That night, after everyone had gone to bed, I sat on the edge of the leather chair that this job had purchased for me. I sat for a couple of hours. The reality of what was happening was sinking in. The kids weren't going to be able to stay in their schools. We weren't going to keep them in the Catholic school system after what had happened. We were going to have to move again. I was now and forever the former athletic director at Dowling that got fired for sending an inappropriate e-mail. This was going to follow us for the rest of our lives. Tears of regret hit the wooden floor. My life, for the most part, had been successful and positive.

I had never had to experience any real heartache or negative consequences. To be on the front page of the paper and the top story on the ten o'clock news was a level of rejection that I had never experienced. But I needed this jolt in order to understand that my way of living was wrong. That night in my living room chair was the moment in my life that I became a completely broken man.

PICKING UP
THE PIECES

We didn't go to church on Sunday, May 21. The kids didn't ask why. May 21 was also our eighteenth wedding anniversary. We didn't celebrate. I didn't even remember it.

Then it was Monday morning without a job. The world kept moving and I was still at home. I was a laughingstock within the internet blogosphere in Iowa. Our Clive, Iowa, neighbors stayed away. A few faculty members at Dowling and my closest friends from high school had called and shared their condolences about me losing my job. Michelle went to work in her home office and I put my golf clubs in my car and went to a driving range. I felt sorry for myself and I didn't know what to do. I thought hitting golf balls would clear my head, but it was a terrible waste of time and made me feel worse.

The next day, I thought about hitting some more golf balls, but I ended up going to a bookstore. Atheism had gotten me here. The brokenness that I felt now was leading me toward a light. I found myself in the section titled "Spiritual" and picked up a book called *Jesus: Life Coach* by Laurie Beth Jones. The sports theme caught my attention. I went home to read.

I started to go to a local park each morning with our dog to walk, run, and think. I started to pray to God. I asked for forgiveness. I found myself wanting to get closer to God instead of farther away from Him.

My career? I wasn't sure if there would be a school that would hire me after a public email fiasco.

After all this publicity, could I be a school administrator again? Michelle and I realized that staying in Des Moines probably wasn't going to happen. We called a realtor. This thing rocked us in many ways.

I ran from God and He pursued me. He helped inflame my attitude toward religion and my job. The circumstances around me, the desires that I had, and that e-mail address on a reply e-mail to my brother capped off the end of my life as a self-centered nonbeliever. My heart was broken. I was a person who was always afraid of failure and always afraid of being seen as a failure. That fear made me wake up in the middle of the night hundreds of times after a dream where I wasn't prepared to teach a geography lesson, or where the other team showed up and I hadn't prepared the baseball field. Public failure, to me, was the worst thing that could happen and it shattered my soul. What happened to me in West Des Moines was a perfectly targeted storm.

Proverbs 21:23 says, "He who guards his mouth and his tongue keeps himself from calamity." I laughed when I first read that because "calamity" is a great word for what happened in West Des Moines in May of 2006.

The same God who whispered my name back at St. Joseph's Church in LeMars had not forgotten about me even though I pushed Him away as hard as I could. In fact, he was standing next to me with his arms open, waiting for my heart to break open and then accept and commit to Him; essentially picking up the pieces of my broken life and gluing them back together. And the truth is, I didn't pick up the pieces … He did.

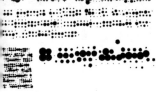

SALVATION

The park that I went to each morning in June of 2006 was actually a set of three slow-pitch softball fields in Clive, Iowa. I would put Benny in the back of the minivan and drive about two miles to the park. Then, I'd run and walk for about forty-five minutes. Several incredibly important things happened to me in those weeks at the park.

I began a routine of prayer and thought. I would start by saying the Lord's Prayer followed by a Hail Mary. That was followed by a prayer to St. Joseph asking him to help us sell our house (an old Catholic tradition that we were still counting on - we had bought the house on Clark Street in Clive with one of those low interest mortgages that got such bad publicity when the economy went bad in 2009) and then I'd talk to my deceased mom. I would tell her how much I loved her and missed her.

One day as I circumnavigated the park, I hit an emotional wall. I was becoming more and more desperate about my life and what was going to happen to our family now that I was road kill on the big city street. The praying and the book that I was reading advanced me spiritually, but there was still a big hole in my heart.

I was finally on the brink of surrendering everything to God. After all my years of denying God's existence and riding the rollercoaster that was my faith life, I stopped in my tracks and put my hands on my knees and closed my eyes. Out loud, I said, "Thank you Lord...for kicking my butt." That was the moment that I surrendered my life to God. I asked Him to forgive me and I asked Him for help. I walked around the softball fields one more time talking to God about everything that was in my heart. The conversation was different now. The connection was real. God finally had my attention and He was now going to get my sincere commitment to Him.

That spiritual event triggered several other events. I got in the car to drive home and found an FM Christian station that was broadcasting Dr. Charles Stanley. He just happened to be talking about how and why God lets bad things happen to people. It was perfect. What great timing. I listened to him for the rest of the summer and still follow him today.

A few early mornings later, at the park, I must have not shut the van hatch all the way after I let the dog out. So after my running and prayer, I went back to the van and the battery was dead. It was about nine in the morning. I knew Michelle would be working so I called my sophomore son Adam and asked him to come to the park with jumper cables. We jumped the car and as Adam got back into his car he pulled out a U2 compact disc and said, "Hey, have you heard this?" I took it and looked at the list of songs as he drove away. It was U2's "How to Dismantle an Atomic Bomb" CD. I saw the last track titled "Yahweh." I listened to it and read the liner notes at the same time. "Yahweh" is one of the most powerful Christian songs that I have ever heard. A dead battery leads to my son tossing me a CD with a song that would be another building block in my spiritual revival. The messages that I was receiving were perfect in their content as well as their timing.

The next week, almost the middle of June, I spotted a homeless man under the canopy of trees that surrounded the park. I stopped running and started thinking. I went to the van to grab my billfold then went to the man and gave him all the money that I had with me saying, "Here is something for you." "God bless you," he said back. I never saw him again. I felt like I had just been tested. The series of events that occurred in the park in June of 2006 were miraculous to me.

My mind was getting on the right track. My spiritual connection was giving me hope.

One afternoon, in those early weeks of June, I got a call from Tom Cooper, then the superintendent at Woodbury Central School in Moville, Iowa. The school where our kids had once gone to school and the town where we had lived for 10 years had an opening for a middle and high school principal and he wanted me to interview. I had applied for an assistant principal job in the Sioux City, Iowa public school district where I had been a teacher, coach, and administrator for nine years (thinking I'd be a shoe-in) but they told me that the e-mail debacle disqualified me from even interviewing.

But the school where my children first went to school in the town we used to live in had an opening and they were calling me…despite my circumstances.

I interviewed in Moville and got the job. I told the school board the entire story of what went down in Des Moines. They showed a lot of confidence in me and I will be forever grateful to Mr. Cooper and the board for hiring me when the vast majority of schools probably wouldn't give me an interview.

We were going to go back to the town we lived in from 1990 to 2000. The blow that our three children had received from the public hanging of their father was softened by the fact that they would be moving back to old friends and a school that they were familiar with. Michelle's mom and her family and friends were clogging God's airwaves with prayers for my family. We had incredible support from the people who loved us.

Our house sold quickly. Instead of losing our shorts with the no down-payment loan, we profited a whopping eighteen dollars!

Michelle was able to keep her job despite the move. Adam and Nolan would end up getting involved in a total of ten extracurricular activities during their first year back.

We found a beautiful Moville home in a great neighborhood.

In setting up our new phone service, the phone company worker on the other side of the line asked, "Do you want your old phone number back?" It had been four years since we had left Moville for what I thought were greener pastures. Getting our old phone number back was like the icing on the cake.

It wasn't fun to pack our house up again and drive out of the big city (the baseball team didn't help us this time) but things came together so quickly and so beautifully after I started a real relationship with Christ. The Apostle Paul wrote in his letter to the Romans, "And we know that in all things God works for the good of those who love Him, who have been called according to His purpose" (Romans 8:28).

My relationship with the Lord was alive and growing and we were definitely better off in this relationship. Atheism has nothing to offer. God, I was finding, offered everything that has real meaning.

I have no doubt that God arranged the demise of my selfish existence and fertilized the life I now lead with love and grace. Things have worked for the good since I started to believe. There's a saying that I love that goes like this: "Religion is for people who don't want to go to hell, and spirituality is for people who have been through it." People who have been broken by circumstances and have responded by seeking God understand what that means.

PIECES OF GRACE

Just about the only happy thought I had in late May 2006, before I asked God to come into my life, was "At least I didn't have cancer, right?" That positively sarcastic thought is what kept me emotionally alive in the hours after the carnage on the ten o'clock news. But one afternoon in the middle of June in our house on Clark Street, I took a shower and, while washing my neck, I felt a hard lump. I just shook my head and mumbled, "No, no, no, no." I didn't tell anyone and kept on moving and hoped it would go away. Michelle wasn't ready to hear from me that I had a rather large lump on what was probably a lymph node.

Four months later, when most of the dust had settled with the new job and life in Moville, I finally told Michelle about the lump, which had gotten a little bigger and was starting to be pretty visible. She touched it and got me into the local medical clinic. I Googled my symptom and began to read about Non-Hodgkin's Lymphoma. The first couple of doctors I saw had a cryptic tone to their voices.

A few days before the surgery that would tell if I had lymphoma, I went to the county fairgrounds near our house and took Benny for a run. As I walked around with the dog, praying for some diagnosis besides cancer, I started, as Forrest Gump would say, "For no particular reason," singing the Beatles tune "Let It Be" with its verses "And in the hour of darkness, Mother Mary comes to me, speaking words of wisdom..." When the walk was over, I went back to the van, put the dog in the back and turned on the engine and radio. "Let It Be," at that exact same point in the song, played through the speakers. I breathed in deeply and felt the comfort that can only come from connecting to and trusting in God. People can call that kind of event a coincidence all they want. But when these "coincidences" happen as you are communicating with God, and their effect is so personally powerful, how can they be interpreted as anything but minor miracles coming from above?

In the surgery prep room at the hospital, minutes from knowing if another life changing event was going to happen to our family, another miracle, of sorts, happened to me. I was lying on the hospital bed with my eyes closed and a bright light above me as Michelle and I listened to the instructions from the nurse. I began to pray, "Jesus walk with me, Holy Spirit help me." Then, a flash went by my closed eyes, like someone had taken their hand and waved it across my face one time. I opened my eyes to see the bright lights above. Michelle and the nurse were ten feet away from me. I didn't think much about the flash at the time.

The doctor sliced my neck open and took the enlarged lymph node out. He said the lump was almost as big as a tennis ball, but it wasn't cancer. It was some type of infection. I was one of three people who had the same lymph node surgery by the same doctor that day. I was the only one who didn't have lymphoma. I came out to the waiting room and Michelle was crying. My faith in Christ continued to grow. My spiritual life was being put together like a puzzle, one powerful piece at a time.

A few months after the surgery, I was flipping channels and started to watch an old black-and-white rerun of one of Billy Graham's stadium revivals from the 1960s. He spoke about how the Holy Spirit can come in a flash in front of our eyes. I remembered my surgery day experience. The Bible says that amazing things, incomprehensible things, will happen when you love and fear God. I pray that these amazing "co-incidences" keep happening in my life.

SANDING THE WOOD

I've heard preachers say, and I've read about how God sands and shapes people who believe in Him. Like a skilled carpenter with a piece of sandpaper, He makes things happen in our lives. He plants thoughts inside our hearts. He brings other people and events into our lives for His purposes and continually shapes us so that we are more and more like Jesus. One of the things Laurie Beth Jones writes about is how she has adopted ladybugs as her spiritual mascot. Whenever she sees a ladybug, she feels God is saying, "I love you and I'm close to you."

As I was reading my first book about building a relationship with God in the summer of 2006, I read Jones's chapter about ladybugs and I looked out the window of our living room and saw a beautiful red northern cardinal. I adopted the cardinal as my spiritual mascot and asked God to help me stay focused by using the redbird as a reminder that God is always with me. Two months later, I walked into the main office at Woodbury Central School in Moville, Iowa and above the head of the superintendent's secretary was a large framed picture of a big, fat male cardinal. Later that morning, I took my first walk down to our counselor's office and I saw that he had a big picture portrait of another cardinal. I chuckled. My old self would scoff at the "coincidence." My new self was energized by the communing nature of everything that was happening to me and around me ...a much better feeling than what cynicism gives you.

Over the last few years, I have bought a lot of birdfeeders. The feeders are filled with black sunflowers seeds. Our record, during the winter, is twelve cardinals, some male and some female, at one time in our backyard sanctuary. It's been an awesome reminder for me of who I am, why I'm here, and how blessed we are as a family.

Then, about a year and a half into my job as the middle and high school principal at Woodbury Central, I got way down. A series of events at school had me a bit depressed and not wanting to pray or read the Bible. I felt like I had lost my connection. We went to our local Catholic church on Saturday night and I knelt in the pew. I put my head down and spaced off for a minute or two. Then I lifted my head up to look forward and there, two pews ahead of us, was an elderly woman wearing a bright white sweater that had a huge embroidered cardinal planted on the back. My spiritual battery was re-charged.

With all these things happening to me how could I not believe in God, Jesus, and the Holy Spirit? My only regret is that it took so long for me to live this life. I regret that it took God having to crush me in order to save me.

His sandpaper is priceless. I pray that He keeps shaping me. The process, as long as I am praying, reading the Bible, and keeping Him close, has been an awesome ride. I have peace and purpose. I feel privileged and blessed to be able to live a life for Him. I know that He is living within me and that if I just let Him work in me, then His plan for my life will be fulfilled. The plan that He has for us is the best plan possible for our lives. We just need to believe and trust.

Here is an amazing fact in my life. Every time, *every time*, that I deal with an issue at home or at work and don't bring God into the equation, it doesn't work out very well. And every time I do bring God in by asking for His guidance and help, *every time* I do that, things seem to work out very well. I've never had so much peace. Life is amazing living connected to God.

THE DESTINY
OF THOSE WHO
FORGET GOD

Once in awhile, I go back to Des Moines for a con-
ference or athletic event. The interstate runs by
Dowling. I look over at the big Catholic school as I
drive by and think about what I really had there and
what I thought I had there. I had what I thought was
a big-time job in a big-time school. Professionally, I
was living my own dream. But it was a job that I had
bull-rushed in my own way without God's approval.
It wasn't going to work out. Our lives don't work out
so well when we're not plugged in to God's will. God
has a plan for everybody. I ran from God's plan for
me in every way that I could. Then a perfect storm
came and picked my family and I up and we landed

in a place a long way from the front porch of a prestigious school in West Des Moines. Small-town Iowa is a long ways from the big city, but in my sweet spot in terms of God's plan for me. The end of my year at Dowling is now a shake-your-head footnote in that school's history…something that the administration there wants to forget, I'm sure. As for me, I never want to forget how I got to the place that I am now.

On that Monday morning after the crash I felt like a fugitive. And then God takes the sandpaper and starts working on me. I think without the Lord in my life, my perceived demotion to a small town and a small school would have been a disaster. Without a relationship with God, I would have been bitter and the downward spiral would have continued into a worse predicament. This place where I spent five post-Dowling years helped make me a better husband, father and school administrator. My natural gifts in terms of how I relate to teenagers have met God's plan for me. This life has led me into a wonderful middle school-only principal job back in LeMars that I'm just beginning as this book is being published. Life is sweet because I have put God number one in my life. Because of that fact, I went from feeling like a fugitive in my own town to feeling tremendous gratitude for another chance to continue in education.

The wife of our town veterinarian asked me one day how things were going since "the thing down there," meaning the debacle in Des Moines. With total honesty, I said, "Helen, I would have that whole thing happen to us again. Moving back here has been the best thing that has ever happened to me." I truly believe that but I also know that our happiness and acceptance of our lives after what we've gone through would be impossible without the grace and love that God has given to us as a family.

Alistair Begg said in a recent sermon, "What a great God; that He comes to us again and again and again ... By the whisper of child, by the loss of a tire on the freeway or by the rising of a great storm, He pursues His wandering child because He loves us so much that He doesn't want to leave us (like Jonah) in the belly of a great fish."[1]

I believe that humans were created with a yearning for God. Our hearts, if not filled by God, have a large void. People go in many different directions in an effort to fill the void. Some people, like me, rationalize God out of their lives completely through atheism. The peace and fullness of the life I am now privileged to lead is a result of my repentance, my surrender to God's will, my acceptance of Jesus as my Savior and my commitment to make God first in my life. I regret that it took a "calamity," but I thank God for having loved me enough to pursue me. For me, this "great storm" *was* the best thing that has ever happened in my life.

In the Bible, the Old Testament life of Job was a little more painful than mine. He was a righteous man with a huge farm and ten kids who threw a lot of parties. God let the devil destroy Job's farm and all his animals and kill all ten of his children in order to test his faith in God. Job responded by saying, "Naked I came from my mother's womb and naked I will depart. The Lord gave and Lord has taken away; may the name of the Lord be praised" (Job 1:21).

Seeing that this didn't break Job's spirit, the devil asks God if he can really put the screws to Job and God permits it. Job then develops painful sores all over his body and he prays that he dies. His friends sit down with him and they discuss hardship and how people who keep faith in God can persevere better than people who don't have faith. One of his friends says something that fits the existence of non-believers:

> Can a papyrus grow tall where there is no marsh?
>
> Can reeds thrive without water?
>
> While they are still growing and uncut, they wither
>
> more quickly than grass.
>
> Such is the destiny of all who forget God;
>
> so perishes the hope of the godless.
>
> What he trusts in is fragile; what he relies on is a spider web.
>
> He leans on his web, but it gives way;
>
> he clings to it, but it does not hold.
>
> Job 8:11-15

Job's friend is talking about the God-implanted need that comes with being a human being. We live best when our soul is filled with His love. And God gives us a foundation of human truth on which to stand and its support can't fail. People who forget God or don't know God don't have the living water that can make their roots strong. We don't need "how-to" books on how to succeed, lose weight or raise kids. Everything that we need to live a good life is contained in God's Word, the Bible. God's words can't fail because they are based on truth...total honesty, love, hope, and what's right for the spiritual, emotional, physical, psychological, and social needs of the human race. You see, without God, we have no *real* hope for the best life.

HE'S NOT DONE YET

I heard God's voice once. I heard it big and loud in my ears at St. Joseph's Church in LeMars another life ago. I have no other explanation that would make sense given everything else that has happened since 2005. Five years after the first time I heard His voice, I heard my first name spoken again in a loud, clear, and rich voice. This time, there wasn't anyone even close to me. It was real and I look at it as an honor and an opportunity. There are many scripture passages and songs about "being called by name." Pastor and author Max Lucado wrote, in his book titled *When God Whispers Your Name*, that when God whispers your name "it reminds you that God is not finished with you yet. Oh, you may think he is. You may think you've peaked. You may think he's got someone else to do the job. If so, think again." [1]

My relationship with Jesus is moving forward. However, I do fail in some way every day. I also have periods of time when I am in the most joyous and peaceful place. God's grace has fallen on my family. My relationship with my wife Michelle is an amazing blessing. She has always been a believer. Her faith and trust in the Lord kept our family together throughout our struggle and she has never stopped loving me and praying for me even as I flopped on the dock like a fish gasping for air. It was her prayers, and the prayers of our family and friends, and God's eternal mercy that saved me.

When we moved to the big city, Michelle got a new job that allowed her to stay home. Her being home when I got booted from the Dowling campus was a huge blessing. Michelle not having to leave the house every day during that summer of transition was a great help to our three kids as well. She was in the house all day everyday keeping us afloat. It was that part of God's plan that helped our family stay focused on loving each other.

Today, I read from the Bible almost every day. I listen to pastors Alistair Begg and Dr. Charles Stanley and read the books of Max Lucado and other Christian authors. Those three Christian leaders make the hair on my neck stand up one minute and make me cry the next. Christian music inspires me and pushes me forward in my walk with Christ. I have learned that I never stand still in my spiritual life. I'm either moving forward or I'm falling backward. I am learning that putting Jesus first in my life has incredible rewards, with inner peace and hope for eternity being at the top of the list.

I never thought I'd write about my life and share it with anyone. But God, indeed, is not finished with me yet. He keeps rubbing me with His gritty sandpaper. It's time for me to start sharing. Maybe I can make a difference for someone.

My hope for anyone who reads this is that you think about your dreams and go for it. Focus on the talents God gave you and live every day with your relationship with God as your first priority. Don't try it alone. Develop your relationship with Jesus and then *hold on tight*. If you trust Him, you will allow Him to work out his plan for your life. Incredible things will happen. I guarantee it because I've experienced it in my own life.

GETTING GOOSEBUMPS

I used to be a "good" Catholic. Well, that's a relative term but I grew up in a happy Catholic home. I not only attended Catholic grade school, junior high, and high school, but was also an administrator in two Catholic schools. If being in good with the Lord was about being in a religious environment, then I was in deep. Yet, even with all religious webbing around me, I fell through the web and landed in the pit. Despite my upbringing, I didn't have a foundation of belief to hold me up. Why did I push God under the carpet? How do people brought up with religion become non-believers?

First, I believe that it is our nature to do what we want to do-to run our own lives and live how the world wants us to live. I wanted to set my own rules. That's pretty normal. Whenever I got close to giving in to God, I got scared of what that commitment would mean in my life and I ran the other way.

With denial came rationalization. I explained my atheism to myself and to a few friends by using science and the theory of evolution. The Bible was just a story. That allowed me to live my life the way I wanted without any guilt.

As I explained earlier, I was also turned off by my brother's ministry. He tried to convert me and I thought he was crazy. I don't think other people can save you. Only God can save us. I believe that all Christians need to share the Gospel and their personal story with non-believers, but we also need to realize that we can't personally save another person. Salvation happens through God's hands, not ours-no matter how hard we might try.

I was also turned off by the hypocrisy that I experienced in the church. God wants us to have an intimate, personal relationship with Him. I don't believe that he needs all the man-made rules and all the human judgment that inherently comes with man-made rules. I don't think that when we give to those less fortunate that we have to bring a camera so that a picture can be sent to the media in order to benefit the organization.

I was also a selfish and ignorant individual who didn't have the courage to follow Christ after being given great opportunities to be close to Him.

I, in many ways, wasted almost forty-four years of my life by not being a close follower of God, Jesus and the Holy Spirit.

If you have doubts of God's existence—if you can't, for the life of you, believe that there is a God who cares deeply for you and has a plan for you—just open up a tiny place in your heart and mind that can stay open to belief. The difference that He has made in my life is:

Night and day.

Dark and light.

I went from fear and negativity to hope and positivity.

I went from being anxious to being peaceful and confident.

You can do this too. I get goosebumps all the time now. Goosebumps happen when you experience strong emotion and your brain's limbic system reacts. The hair follicles around your body rise up because something powerful is happening around you or in you.

I used to get goosebumps when I taught a great lesson in the classroom and the kids "really got it" through their involvement in the lesson. I used to get goose bumps in high school baseball practice and games when a skill that I had taught was executed successfully in a live scrimmage or in a game. Now, I get goosebumps through a scripture reading, a song, a powerful sermon or a situation where God's hand touches my heart. I get goose bumps when what I'm saying, doing, seeing, or hearing is in God's wheelhouse, or will, for me. It's an awesome feeling.

You can have this feeling too. All you have to do is believe, trust, and put Him first in your life.

Many people, along with sixteenth-century theologian John Calvin, believe that a person won't know who they really are until they know who Jesus is. I believe that. *And when you really know who Jesus is, then you will find yourself in a growing personal relationship and your life will begin to flow in a tremendously positive way.* That doesn't mean bad things won't happen to you. It does mean that you will realize that all of the things that happen according to God's will for you will grow you as a Christian. Your life experience, in turn, will be full, meaningful and satisfying.

OF SALMON
AND SUCH

The way I see things now, there are two kinds of people in relationship to the world of Christianity. There are those people who are trying to live their lives in their own strength. They see everything, from relationships to the workplace, as something they have to handle personally. They rely on themselves for all things important in their lives. If you are one of these people (and I was), you are like a fish swimming upstream against the current. Life is going to be a struggle (all of the time for some, and at some point, inevitably, for others) because you are trying to do it on your own, against the rushing water that the world throws at us.

People who have accepted Jesus as their savior and have surrendered everything, from relationships to their careers, to God, have a whole different life. Because of God's grace, these people are swimming downstream with the power of God helping them along. Death, disease and heartache still happen to saved Christians but their faith and trust in God changes their attitudes and perceptions. Pain becomes an opportunity to get closer to God. Fear becomes a chance to surrender. It's a new and fantastic life.

Pride (I can handle this myself!) and selfishness kept me from seeing the truth of our existence here on earth. It took a storm for me to become broken to a point where I surrendered to God. It doesn't have to come to that for you.

In the Gospel of Luke, Jesus says:

> If anyone would come after me, he must deny himself and take up his cross daily and follow me. For whoever wants to save his life will lose it, but whoever loses his life for me will save it. What good is it for a man to gain the whole world, and yet lose or forfeit his very self?
>
> Luke 9:23-25

Don't try to swim upstream like a salmon, against the current of the world, on a quest for survival and success. True success comes when we give in and realize that Jesus *is* the rushing current that flows toward true happiness, fulfillment and heaven. Trust in God and swim downstream.

AFTERWORD

My Little Cinderella

Back to the Father-Daughter dance, where I was preoccupied with work instead of my own beautiful fourth-grade princess. Christian songwriter Stephen Curtis Chapman wrote an incredible song about his young daughter Maria, who died in a tragic accident soon after the song was written. It's a song about not taking life for granted. The lyrics hit home with me because they sum up my feelings for my daughter. It also describes Cara's tremendous enthusiasm to be with her Dad as well as what was happening the night I took her to the dance.

> *"She spins and she sways,*
> *To whatever song plays,.*
> *Without a care in the world,*
> *And I'm sitting here wearing*
> *The weight of the world on my shoulders.*

It's been a long day,
And there's still work to do.
She's pulling at me
Saying 'Dad, I need you'

There's a ball at the castle
And I've been invited
And I need to practice my dancing
'Oh, please, Daddy, please?'

So I will dance with Cinderella
While she is here in my arms
'Cause I know something the prince never knew
Oh, I will dance with Cinderella
I don't want to miss even one song
'Cause all too soon the clock will strike midnight
*And she'll be gone..."*1

Sweetheart, I promise that I won't miss another dance.

Cara and I at the Holy Trinity Father-Daughter Dance
February 2006

ENDNOTES

The E-mail

1. Alistair Begg, "The Man Who Said No" (Truth for Life & Parkside Church Sermon), October 21, 2009.
2. Alistair Begg, "The Man Who Said No" (Truth for Life & Parkside Church Sermon), October 21, 2009.

The Destiny of Those Who Forget God

1. Alistair Begg, "The Man Who Said No" (Truth for Life & Parkside Church Sermon), October 21, 2009.

He's Not Done Yet

1. Max Lucado, When God Whispers Your Name, (Nashville TN. Thomas Nelson, Inc. 1999), p. 17.

Afterword

1. Cinderella. Words and Music by Stephen Curtis Chapman © 2007 Sparrow Song (BMI) and PRIMARY WAVE BRIAN (CHAPMAN SP ACCT) (BMI) SPARROW SONG Admin. At EMICMGPUBLISHING.COM

All Rights Reserved Used by Permission
Reprinted by Permission of Hal Leonard Corporation